STUCK

POETRY BOOK DESCRIPTION

"Stuck" explores the intricate facets of human experience. Through its verses, it delves deep into the struggle with mental health, portraying the often-turbulent journey individuals face in this regard. It also touches upon the theme of spiritual attacks, offering a poetic lens through which to view these internal battles.

"Stuck" doesn't shy away from the complexities of relationships with friends and the broader spectrum of people we encounter daily. It weaves a narrative around the challenges and joys of these connections, inviting readers to reflect on their own interpersonal experiences.

Laziness, a common human trait, is another theme artfully explored within the pages of *"Stuck."* The poems resonate with those who have experienced the pull of inertia while harboring dreams and aspirations of greatness. It underscores the struggle to overcome procrastination and complacency.

At its core, *"Stuck"* is an inspirational work that encourages readers to confront their mental health challenges head-on and find their authentic strength. It's a poetic journey that offers solace and motivation, reminding us all that growth and self-discovery are achievable, even in the face of life's most daunting obstacles.

By Nu Pink The Writer

POET, SONGWRITER, AND ALCHEMIST

Follow me on all social media platforms

@bynupinkthewriter

DEDICATION

To Me, Myself, and God

ACKNOWLEGEMENT

To the friends I had
To the men I liked
To the mother I loved
To the people who misunderstood

Thank you!

STUCK

Silence is the art of listening
Hearing the earth whispering
I go deep within, awakening my spirit
The person I knew used to be daring
She seeks no one, only the one in the mirror
Time faded, time came, time has left
Years passed, years progressed
What happened, she wants to know

I've changed for the weak
I am not the person I used to be
I forget who I am when I'm not at ease
I've listened to others instead of
the woman I used to see

TABLE OF CONTENTS

TABLE OF CONTENTS

TABLE OF CONTENTS

"We need each other,
but how can we truly love one another
when the ego is the one we trust."

By NuPink The Writer

KIND

My heart sits sleeveless, ready to give

I love with wide arms; I love without fear

My kindness is the source of my being

Sometimes, it's too much to bear

Unrequited love makes me anxious

Brotherly love, I give gracefully

I tend to love without knowing it

Being kind is how I show it

It's an unhealthy behavior, I take ownership

It feels good, it fills up my soul

Avoidance, maybe, I'm avoiding my ego

Is my kindness the reason I feel hurt?

Could I be avoiding myself to appease others?

Selfishness versus selflessness

A battle I must come to terms with

I am losing every chance I get

Because I don't believe I am a good person

Unless I keep giving to prove I'm worth it

NOTE TO SELF #1

Being kind is not an obligation; it's a privilege.
If someone takes your kindness for granted, it's their loss

CHANGE

Comfortability became imperative
A need for content
becomes the fear of evolution
I buy things to fill the void
I cannot wait because I am spoiled
I lack patience for myself and The Lord
Greatness has a tendency of knocking
I hear it; it lightly taps my door
I fear judgment when I answer
I open with speculations,
I tell myself I deserve it
But my ego has reservations
I am a victim of greed and lust
I am a sinner because I lost trust
God is with me, but I still feel stuck
Hesitation, but I am chosen
It's the need to change, I am stressing
I know I am destined for greatness
I need to awaken and have patience
But I am too comfortable in the matrix

GUILTY

Dark angel,
suppose it's me
I've been here for a while
Haven't done much
Just living this life
I have cried
They have shouted
Many done left
Many never forgave
Pointed the finger
Made me Satan
I am the villain
Guilty of all charges
I blame myself

I am guilty of whatever you believe I have done.

ENEMY

I am a star, but my light went dark

In the shadows of human thoughts

They casted spells, I embarked

The depression to their hurting

The anxieties of their worries

I lowered my frequency for their glory

I believed their words and their stories

Every lie they told; I took ownership

Every thought they stated I embedded

I became the person which was them

Now I must say, they have won

MYSELF

I question myself

I question my faith

I don't understand

I don't feel equate

Everyone had love

Yet, I'm not enough

I grounded myself

I spent time knowing myself

Yet, there's stagnant movement

Is there a psychological rule to it?

Mortality, in actuality,

Inability to love effectively

Do I really love me?

Like, really like me?

Be the second to none

But I'm second to one

Myself.

STUCK

MIRROR

I miss you

I stared in the mirror

Again, it's my reflection

"Hi, self."

There's no response

Just a smirk

I look closely

I see all my flaws

Ugh! I look awful

I need to drink more water

But I don't, I love my sweets

Ugh! Look at my teeth

I know there are cavities

Tooth decay, probably

I need to do better

I need to feel better

Ugh! I'm going back to bed

I'll see you later

THE TRAIL

A long path to nowhere
Well, that's what I thought
When I walked down the trail of growth
The longest journey I ever fucking walked
The need for change was slow and stagnant
Highly independent, I attracted the unbalance
The pessimists, the chiefs of negativity, the needy
Yet, I gave without any regard, without any reasons

A lonely walk I have walked
No guidance, just my feet stepping
I must trust in myself, but where to go?
Prosperity is what I deserve
Yet, I'm still scared of my own love

IMPOSER SYNDROME

Resistance toward the inner being

The spirit of others affects my seeing

The strength from my intuition has weakened

I want to believe in me, yet I'm scared of me

I see me, but I am afraid of being authentically me

I'll enter the room with positivity, a feeling of divinity

Yet, I'll feel the mood swings

Am I crazy or just moody?

Who am I when I am alone?

Am I someone no one actually knows?

The perception from other's eyes

Are telling me I am not their kind

I try my best to be congenial

Fit in, be a part of the norm

Yet, I questioned my ego

"Why do you want to be likable?"

NOTE TO SELF #2

Be the eyes who see you first.
Soon you will receive the love you always deserved.

STUCK

QUALMS

The oppression of my being is killing me

A cycle of patterns, unlearned mistakes is taunting me

Cannot heal, cannot see beyond the past or the future

In my mind, life rewinds, fast-forward, yet I'm still clueless

The present time hasn't been gifted but wicked

The days I live, are the days I sin

I ask myself, why are you idle?

The question never got its answer

I sit here, on the edge of the bed,

Wondering...

If my limps can move

as I move my foot

Why can't I?

Mentally, I can't

I am tired.

LACK

It's the inability to move, knowing I can
Yet, I lay here with no motion
Even though,
I grab my phone and start strolling
The thought of moving, I lack the motives
Sleepily, I never went to sleep with ease
Awakening, I am awakened but not ready
I lack; I'm still sleepy
Mentally, I think to move
But laziness makes me comfortable.

STUCK

BED

Dreamland, a place I love to go when life is boring

I will sleep tight until God says, *"WAKE UP!"*

Aw damn, it's daylight!

The birds are chirping

The sun has awakened

I slept, but still exhausted

Lethargic, I start yawning

Am I depressed or something?

I questioned myself as I sat on the edge of the bed

My feet are touching the cold wooden floor

Damn, I'm cold

I lay back down

I love my bed and pillows

I just want to rest here

Be awakened to my reveries

Please, life, leave me alone

Let me just rest and be at home

STUCK

I DREAM

Every day, I dream

Drift off, immerse in my thoughts

I pray and make wishes in the dark

Hoping my future self agrees with me

I channel my reality when asleep

In my mind, I feel alive

Funny and witty, clever but silly

My friends, my family are lauding

I dream peacefully, refusing to get up

I visualize every wish I prayed for

Manifesting my future, but I'm stuck

In my bed, I lie awake; I'm still not up

I dream, I dream like Martin Luther King.

I dream I dream, I only have a dime and a dream.

I dream I dream, but I have no energy to live my dreams

GET UP

Eyes open wide

Another day, another dime

I am up, ready to waste time

What to wear? Ugh!

This decision triggers my anxiety

Do I want to look fly today?

Or *FINE*, today?

How do I feel?

TIRED TODAY!

I just want to go back to sleep

Get up and do nothing

But I must do something

I have a purpose

I must awaken it

Shake off this laziness

And go to work… today.

NOTE TO SELF #3

Motivation isn't technical.

It is the willingness to pursue.

You're stuck because you live in comfort.

You've lost the drive to improve.

It's okay to rest, but baby, you need to get up.

You have a purpose, like the people you see on TikTok.

OKAY

A world of hurt

Scars from self-harm

I afflict the pain

To my bruised skin, but I'm okay

Trust me, I am okay

I hide behind this smile; I exude

It's a force I learned to pretend

It's a power I urge to end

I won't because I can't

It eases my intense emotions

It assuages the qualms

I know I am strong

I know I am stoic

I can hurt physically

Without anyone noticing

That I am not okay

Inspired by Netflix Ginny and Georgia Season II

ACQUIESCENCE

Their thumb is on mine's
My strength has forfeit
I succumb to the nonsense
I live in darkness

Their perception is my identity
Their laughter is my self-doubt
I believe what they see
I am who they say I am

I have no power
I rely on them cowardly
I am a child, a folly, a sheep
Someone with low self-esteem
I need guidance; I need direction
I rely on those who are weak but brawn
I am scared because I am not as strong

CONTROL

The power of them

Conquers the me

I hear the mocks

I hear the tease

I feel the woes

I feel unease

I have a choice

I have the will

I know I am smart

I know I am wise

No control

Unowned ropes

I pull, they tug

A battle of selves

Who has the biggest ego?

Is it me?

Or is it them?

EGO

Pinch the nerve

Be my mask

Hide the weakness

Hide my worries

I am strength

I am charm

When you toss

I throw it back

I am pride

I am scorned

I will hurt

I will think

Revenge competes

Revenge defeats

It is ego

It is not me

STUCK

DOUBT

The moment I feel unsure

Is the moment I am uncertain

Second-guessing my choices

Many what-ifs, many maybes

I am dubious; I'm always in doubt

Confusion, there are too many clouds

The uncertainties cause anxiety

The anxiety causes unsurety

What should I do?

Again, I ask my ego.

BALANCE

The ego can be bigger than God

Or as small as a mustard seed

It depends on our confidence

It depends on our self-esteem

How we feel about ourselves matters

How we see ourselves may contradict

Being prideful is one of the deadly sins

Yet, we need ourselves to get up and win

Too much of anything will cause addiction

Too much idleness goes against the ministry

We need to find balance in everything we begin

Having time for those who love us from within

Having time for ourselves to replenish the skin

We need to find balance in everything we touch

Giving back to those who don't have much

Showing love to those who haven't felt a hug

We need to find balance between spirituality and earth

We need to find balance between our soul and our ego

NOTE TO SELF #4

Soul is the DNA of God
Ego is the flesh of the world
What drains your self-esteem?
What feeds your self-importance?
Whatever is your answer is…
Is what you need to heal and let go of?

ON ANOTHER NOTE:
The ego is the author of your story
But the soul will be the reason you share it.

PERFECT

Immaculate

Precisely, intricate

Marvelous

No errs

No pimples

Symmetry

Every part of you

Is perfect

I wish I were perfect

Perfect without makeup

Perfect without flaws

Perfect without foibles

Appeasing to the eyes

Appeasing to the ears

Appeasing to the touch

I wish I were confident enough to say…

I AM ENOUGH.

ILLNESS

It's an illness I owned
Detect and call home
My solar plexus is bound
The energy has debloated
But my abdomen remains swollen

In the physical realm, I'm healthy
Spiritually, I'm battling constantly
Fight or flight, autopilot or manually
I risk it all when I'm my own enemy

My health is inconclusive.
Checkups, examinations
Nothing is found; is it mental?
Or am I spiritually losing it?

Inspired by TikTok @bigtajjj

RUN

Resistance became a friend

I never knew how much I enforce shit

The battle I comply with

I run toward overthinking,

wanting things in my favor

Run away from faith

Thinking things will still fall into place

I became a part of the underachievers

The wishful thinkers, the believers

We will fall, but we will rise in our heads

But in our lives, we're just nobodies

We run and run, just to fall again

Run away from God from within

And keep running until we win

But we will never win because

we're always running.

CYCLE

Around and around, I go
Not happy, but I am on a merry-go
Dizzy, unsure of my purpose
Vertigo, I'm falling, and I lost focus
I've been here before, I remember
Deja rêvé, a precedent moment
What have I learned?

Nothing

As I lie on the carpet flooring,
in time, I will get up again
As anxiety keeps me up again
I love to overthink, overanalyze
Calculating, every fucking thing
But still remain paralyzed
Insanity is becoming the norm
Over and over again, I'll go
Hamster wheeling it
As time isn't mine's
But a cycle.

STUCK

PRESENT

Please don't bother me, I'm thinking

The words are in my vision

They are singing and then crying

They are fighting and then dancing

I pictured them, the past, the future

My strengths, my hunger

My ideas, my desires

I see them, I hear them

I smell them, I feel them

I vibrate low, then high

I feel mid, I feel tired

Now I am present, *"Oh, Hi!"*

You smiled, and I waved

Then you walked away

Without a bye

I remained seated.

Damn, reality is boring

I'd rather dream

than to be present

It's my story.

STALE

It gets old

Time enters life

Here we are

Idle, declining

Getting older

Suffering, surviving

Waiting until the night falls

Again, I sleep

Wake up, repeat

It happens again & again

Older, I get older

Is the less time I have

to be stuck in worrisome

NOTE TO SELF #5

Remembering the past is to learn from the mistakes but never dwell on what was. Be at peace for what is.

HOMOSPIRITUALITY

I am who I attract
The belief I have
The people I meet
Is what I seek
I couldn't see

Accountability, I spoke loosely,
Gave frequently, without knowing
Now I reap what I'm sowing
Shadow working, I didn't deserve pain
But I accept the hurting

They kept coming
I was never a victim
An accomplice to my unhealing
Now I see they weren't the villains
I was unhealed, living in self-affliction.

Inspired by TikTok: @anointedfire

IMPATIENT

The complexity of wanting

Force the non-existing

Here I am needing, being resisted

Fixate on many, not on one thing

Releasing is optional

Rather than facing obstacles

But here I am enforcing shit

Being stubborn, endorsing shit

Applying, molding, coding

I'm in control of all things

Yet, I cannot stay focused

Being impatient will cost me.

COST

I lost so much

In mind, I talk too much

I overthink; I am too much

I give a lot, but it's not enough

It's cost to be in love

It's cost to be loved

A cost I cannot afford

Yet, here I am, giving more than I am served

Yet, here I am, being frivolous, and it hurts

A cost they cannot buy

A cost I cannot tame

In the dark, I count all my ones

In the light, I count all my ones

I always end up short, not by surprise

I always end up depressed; I am not fine.

DESPERATION

Desperation becomes hindrance

I want it so badly; it's resisting

Pulling forward, I want to hold it

Impatient, therefore, it's not coming

I am fixated, navel-gazing on the need

Adamant to buying and having things

Quenching the need to feel accepted

The ego is winning as the soul is sleeping

Materializing my life is my being

Identifying my whys yet I excuse them

What I buy fulfills my cravings

Yet I want more and more; I need it

But do I really need it?

Letting go can be victorious

Yet here I am wanting it, and

being desperate.

Inspired by Comedian Leslie Jones
Talk with Laverne Cox

STUCK

NERVOUS

Scared, mortified

on the verge of crying

My system has an overload

Too many feelings

Too many thoughts

Too much pressure

Too much force

I don't want to be here

Yet I am here

I force myself not to be scared

"Be calm nerves, be calm."

I close my eyes, and then I speak

"Take ya time, now release "

The words are partying in my head

Forming a sentence is torture when I'm red

I relax, take another deep breath

I cannot do this, I'll shut down, I need to rest

My nerves have conquered my confidence

Scared, mortified, now anxious

Leave me alone

I quit.

STUCK

PERPLEXED

This is a pivotal moment. I have a chance to speak
Uttering out whatever is bothering me
Yet, I cannot formulate the words to say
I know what's on my mind, but I cannot convey

My intuition isn't working like it used to
I have to live to know what I am doing
Discernment is intuitive, experience from mistakes
Yet the lessons are unclear, and I cannot vindicate

You asked a question; I am not ready to answer
I'd rather you never asked then to think cleverly
Finding the right choice of words redirects my purpose
How I respond denotes who I am as person

I am an overthinker; imagination is my comfort
I am a homebody; I'd rather live within than publicly
I am nervous; I hate questions that pertain to me
My mind goes wonky when I try to speak

MISCONSTRUE

Think before you speak
I seem to speak then to think
My words are heard but not comprehended
It's misheard by those with selective hearing
Uncertainty, unsurety, I'll stutter, I'll ramble
I am nervous, confused, trying to sound smart
I eventually shut the fuck up once their eyes go dark
I am talking too much subconsciously; I cannot stop
I love to talk when the conversation is deep-seated
I love to hear viewpoints, opinions, and theories
But when it comes to me, no one hears me
When they do, they misconstrue.

STUCK

NEURODIVERGENT

Neither here nor there, I understand. I digress.

Invested in this convo, I speak out of context.

I think uneasily; my words aren't definite.

Watch my actions when I speak up

Nervously, I am self-conscious

Listen to the correction when there's a retrospect

I will realize I said the wrong word, the wrong meaning

I meant to say something more profound, more in-depth

The way I think isn't usual but spiritually intuitive

I don't know everything, but I know by experience

I observe, I listen, I rely on my own instinct

I visualize, I recall, this isn't making sense to me at all

I comprehend yet don't innerstand.

They speak to me in fragments.

Beating around the bush, no transparency

I don't understand, yet I tried to give an opinion

Maybe the facts aren't factual; there's no truth to it

I started questioning everything that was once said

I need details; why are you being evasive?

Gaslighting my opinions as if you were honest

And this is why I try my best to remain silent.

NOTE TO SELF #6

Silence is bliss!

COMFORTABLE

If you believe it, you can achieve it

So why am I stuck?

Playing tug & war with fight or flight

Being the crisis of my pride

It's an issue, let's wonder

Imagine the thoughts

Featuring the reveries

A fantasy, a made-up reality

I seek in my mind

I see it clearly

Abundance of love

Abundance of money

House of fun

House of family

It's a dream of mine's

But can it come true?

Yes, maybe so

Yet, I am contented with…

The same ol,' same ol'

STUCK

RUNAWAY

I was too afraid to run away
So, I had left my reality mentally
Creating characters, creating images
Creating stories, creating false realities
I daydream in my bed as my life slips away
I've lived already; in my head, I found solace
ADHD and depression created this paralysis

I ran away at twelve and never returned
I've been sleeping since then and have yet to wake up
Sleeping beauty, I've been rejuvenating and dormant
Reality was never my present but a punishment
Just surviving, making ends meet while smiling
Because I do not live here, I come to visit, then
mentally disappear.

Inspired by Tik Tok @alliepriestley
Maladaptive Daydreaming

MORAL WORTH

Am I worth it, morally?

Have my good deeds exceeded?

Do others even like me for me?

Or solely for my kind green hands?

Damn, it bleeds!

I love God

I love being given

I want to be accepted

A good spirit who's attentive

But who am I convincing?

The wounded child whose mom screams

"You're spoiled rotten and ungrateful."

Or the reflection I see when I hurt a friend

because they hurt me?

BURDEN

It's like needles and thorns

Tacks, nails

A pinch by a toddler

It hurts, it burns

It's annoying

I know I am

Problems, trouble waters

I tell my stories

No one cares

To hear my worries

They're not intrigue

They're not engross

I am a burden

Leave me alone

STUCK

LOVE

I give without motive

I see beyond the surface

I love because I want it

Yet my love isn't important

Many show me it isn't worth it

HATE

I despised my being

Pour out my misery

My dismay,

my degradation

I give grief,

I give unbalance

I want to love

But I'd rather hate

Showing love

can cause hate

This society sucks!

No one loves

only make ingrates

So, I hate.

MISANTHROPE

It was never the good ones

Always the rude and boor ones

The inconsiderate and controlling ones

The ones who made me feel less than human

The ones who cannot confess and be truthful

They always blame, undermine, and use psychology

Causing me to think I need meds, therapy

I hate humans

Not the ones with empathy

Not the ones who see me

But the ones who hurt me

Intentionally, constantly

Regularly, on the daily

For their self-gratification

They're selfish, they're mean

They're evil-spirited, they reek

FRIENDS

Trusted heart

I ran to whoever loved

Accepted my pain

Accepted my thoughts

Accepted my love

Yet, it was a façade, a game

Did my friends change?

Or am I still the same?

Refusing to see what is

Oblivion, no vigilance

Their potential, I saw their ability

Their light, I saw their brightness

I smiled when they were admired

I clapped when they were honored

But when it was my turn,

there were excuses, empty promises,

and violin music.

STUCK

FRIEND

I love being a "friend."

I'll give, I'll support

We'll laugh, we'll joke

But sometimes

My friendship isn't reciprocal

Many have left me in the cold

Many have reopened closed wounds

Many always saw me as a foe

An enemy to their ego

Someone who just doesn't know

Therefore, I just don't know

Maybe I should stay to myself

Give more time to my art

Be caring to my heart

And be my own friend

My own spark.

NOTE TO SELF #7

Whoever becomes your friend will be blessed.
Heighten your standards and exert your boundaries.
Continue to be kind and loving; you will align with
the right beings, it's all in divine timing.

STUCK

LUSTING

A sinner, I sin

I forgot who I am

I allow other spirits to be vocal

They made me question my motive

I want love, but I remain unfocused

I seek validation instead of a real lover

I quench dopamine and oxytocin

I became obsessed with the thought

I think of the body but not the heart

I think of the sex but not the spirit

I now realize I never wanted love

I lusted to avoid myself

Inspired by TikTok @anoinedfire

UNREQUITED LOVE

Conditional

Fidelity is difficult

We preach, then curse

We're in heat, then hurt

It's torn, it's love

I want more; you give less

I am stuck but contented

I am here in your bed

Your love is solely sex

I think I calculate

Ways to be impactful

Ways to love you better

You distance your spirit

I chase to feel the feeling

You choose another being

I am stuck to the fantasy

I cannot unsee it.

DESERVING

He's loving me

The only one loving on me

I am giving more than I should

He comes over to get what he could

I take it off, knowing I shouldn't, but I still do

He comforts me while I am lonely and forlorn

I like him too much, but I am deserving of more

I can feel it every night when he walks out the door

I am in need of more, I crave for more, I want more

Yet, I keep accepting less than what I am deserving of

NO EFFORT

The likeness of being wanted
is unlikely at the moment
You caged your heart and think with logic
You left me alone to teach me silence
I realize I'm unwanted because it's too quiet
There's no effort, no work, no words, no call
But there's me showing up to every inkling of love
Until I realized there was never none
I decided to pay attention
Follow your lead and be a has-been
Now, you're showing up urging me to speak
I decided to leave you alone
You weren't meant for me.

NOTE TO SELF #8

You are not an option or a pity party.
You shouldn't be loved by default, only by sincerity.

STUCK

NO

I say NO!

That's all you need

Why are you forcing me?

I am not you, you're not me

I have a mind of my own

I am not a dummy

What works for me

Works for me

It's my intuition

What I like is my discretion

Don't force me

Don't coerce me

I am my own person

I said, NO!

PATIENCE

Time once was slow
Younger me watched it go
Tick, tock, tick, tock
I cannot wait to grow up
I wished I had waited to grow up
I wished I enjoyed every moment
I was young and innocent
Mother made me feel less than
Made me feel like a burden
Being a runaway was my motive
But I never dared to do so
I was a child; I was helpless
My past isn't my future
I can run or stay idle
I can jump or be lazy
Or I can simply have patience
Replace time with perseverance
Craft my art, make time for healing
And patiently be me.

DEATH ROW

Innocent mind, innocent eyes

Innocent smile, innocent whys

Embedded pain, embedded anger

Embedded shame, embedded fear

Cursed heart, cursed thoughts

Cursed love, cursed scars

The dark shadow of trauma will find its home

Embedded in your subconsciousness, it'll sow

Your reactions stem from it; how you love comes from it

Self-affliction is hidden, malice spirits manifest it

They saw your light, dimmed it, to content their sight

You were young and naïve, impressionable, and docile

You were demons' prey; you were their push-and-play

Mental illness has now consumed you,

You're helpless and too afraid

You became a prisoner, a cellmate

A lost soul, a confused bird

You're no longer a child but an adult

We cannot stay in comfort

We'll forever be on death row

Let's heal and grow,

And become love and not the hurt.

THE REASON

Behaviors, actions
Demeanor, habits
We do things
We say things
We act a certain way
Teaching and loving
Cultivating and learning
It's in our thought process
It conforms us, it comforts us
Hobbies and passion
Joking and laughing
I need love,
I have compassion
There's no reason
I am simply happy.

FIGHT OR FLIGHT

The thoughts appear
but the pictures are unreal
Yet, it consumes my being
Who I am, who is I?
I see my reality.
I refuse to take responsibility
It's God, it's the devil
I am fearful, but a rebel
I fight, but then I settle
Hopeless but grateful
What the fuck?
I guess I don't know.
Living to survive, surviving to live
I am wasting time but shortening my life.
Working, day and night
Working, night to day
If I sit in stillness, I live in the present
Yet I tell myself, you're being lazy
I need money, so again, I'm working
Making ends meet, but is my soul happy?

EXCUSES

Excuses are only suitable for those who used them

Subconsciously, I keep creating them

Giving myself any reasons to stay stuck

I cannot sing; no one will listen

Studio time is hella expensive

I hate my voice; it's off-pitch

Music enthusiasts have judged

Disappointments, I hate to have them

I become discouraged every time, ugh!

STUCK

ATTACKS

I've been cutting off people
Making my inner circle cleaner

I've been letting go
pushing forward
Being aware of who is for me

I've been changing
spiritually upgrading
Shadow working, finding my identity

Yet, I feel the attacks
The memories, the nostalgia
The urge of reviving the past
But I cannot; I'll relapse
I need to change, grow up
I cannot be the same
But my energy is being missed
I feel it because I've been exhausted.

THE

The answer

The results

I beg to differ

I pause

The idea

The thought

I refuse

I sought

The wrong

The inaccuracy

I find mistakes

I find anomaly

The decision

The fear

Again

I am scared

The lights

The views

This is the life I choose.

WHAT TO DO?

I walk on the Earth's land

What is my purpose?

I stare at the Earth's sand

I live in confusion

I sit in stillness

There were many no's

Yet my heart always said yes

Torn between the two

I remained hopeless

I fear the souls here

Tormented by my own spirit

Stardust has fallen, I follow

Synchronicities and numbers

I see them, and I wondered

What does it all mean?

Will my life be abundant?

Am I chosen?

An alien superstar?

What to do, Lord?

I need to know.

THE CALL

Deep within, she keeps urging me to be free

I keep telling her it's better to write than to sing

She keeps pinching and begging me please

I keep telling her it isn't safe, stay within me

She keeps telling me it'll be okay, we will see

I keep telling her, no, we won't, we will bleed

She keeps saying, let's have faith just to see

Honestly, I am scared as fuck to live in my dreams

I've been judged and ridiculed for being me

She said I know…

Let's do it.

Fuck the no's

Let's sing!

GOD

Who is God?

Is God a reflection of our being?

Or a spirit to our believing?

A question I summoned

sometimes I wonder

The thoughts of others

Who do they perceive…

when they stared closely?

A person who is not sane

Or a person who is Satan?

I observe the lightness of others

I see their aura, and I want to follow

Yet I am told I can't sit with them

Therefore, here I am God

Why am I being outcasted again, Lord?

I sit in stillness; a word of clarity alters my hearing

I feel the positive entity surrounding me

Is my mind playing tricks on me?

Or is God telling me something interesting?

THE TRAIL (SOUL)

A long path to nowhere
Well, that's what I thought
I am seeing a change in how I think
I am conscious of what I say who I speak to
It's not easy, but I am learning and owning
It's not who I was; it's now who I'm becoming
Affirmation is serving; I can now say I'm worth it
What was mental was a gift to my current self
Understanding that I am different
And it's a blessing to be no one else
My reality wasn't from God
but what I thought of myself
I cannot blame source
only the person I choose not to help
What I believe is, is what I become
What I declare will manifest as said
Who I am is someone I am getting to know
My path wasn't to nowhere; it was to my soul.

SEVEN YEARS

Mirror, mirror
Do you see me?
The lover, the healer
The singer, the creator

Mirror, mirror
Can you hear me?
The pain, the blame
The shame

Were you cracked?
Curse for seven years?
Did I hurt your mama's back?

Were you covered?
I've wiped you off.
Here's a damped cloth

Are you okay, mirror?
Are you okay?
It's been seven years
And nothing has changed
We're still the same

STUCK

Having doubt with faith

How insane?

We both know we're great

Who's to blame?

Them or our name

I know it's hard

But our mind is convincing us

Adversity made it tough

Or is it bad luck?

It's us!

We're in the way of self

We are enough

We have everything we need

We need to live in reality

Awaken, my dear

Awaken, you're healed

Awaken, I'm here

Awaken!

NOTE TO SELF #9

Your stress was never yours
Your dismay was never yours
Your worries were never yours
Your ideology for self was never yours

Others made you,
Others deceived you
Others questioned your identity
Others made you feel weak and sorry

You were always beautiful
You were always intelligent
You were always a gift to humankind

Your trauma isn't yours
but a seed to blossom, a seed to grow

MY STORY

STUCK

 I want to extend my heartfelt gratitude to all of you who have taken the time to read "Stuck" and join me on this extraordinary journey.

I've never had it easy, despite what you might see on the surface. For years, I've been struggling with depressive episodes. At times, I've prayed I didn't exist. However, the God in me always kept me above water.

My name is Chevel, but you may know me as Velly Vel on stage and NuPink The Writer as my pen name. I was born in London, England, on November 17, 1991, to a Jamaican mother and an English father. At 2, my mother decided to leave England with me and my Down-Syndrome older brother to Trenton, NJ. Because of this sudden move, my father was absent throughout my upbringing.

With no family support, moving to Trenton was a struggle for us. We were unhoused most of my younger years. We lived with friends of my mother, short-term efficiencies, and, at times, motel rooms. Eventually, my mother got accepted to subsidizing housing when I was 9. We stayed there until I was 18.

STUCK

My school life was also quite challenging. I often felt like an outsider. I endured teasing and emotional torment due to having a lazy eye and speaking differently from my peers. I didn't mind it at first because I knew I was different. However, my mother's high expectations and whimsical behaviors made it worse.

At 6, I used to draw. My mom, brother, and myself, but strangely, I scribbled myself out. Unknowingly, this is when my depressive episodes began.

I was primarily alone since my brother couldn't communicate due to his disability. Consequently, I played and talked to myself. When I was 8, I began singing around the house and crafting songs. I even wrote one down, but when I returned days later to complete it, I had forgotten the melody. I stopped songwriting.

My journey into poetry began at 12. I was grappling with intense emotions and needed an outlet. The challenges at school and home became even more overwhelming as I entered middle school. I was subjected to name-calling and verbal bullying and became a target for the class clowns. I was just too afraid to stand up for myself.

My peers were delinquents and hoodrats, and my mother constantly threatened me about misbehaving in school, which frightened me into submission. Poetry and daydreaming became my lifeline. Both helped me cope with the overwhelming emotions, and that's when I started songwriting again.

At 17, I inadvertently became the sole breadwinner during my summer break. I made an innocent mistake by opening a checking account with my second check. My check was dated to be clear the following week. My mom was furious and physically kicked me out. I went to stay with my best friend and her family. Three weeks before I turned 18, my mother found me, and I reluctantly had to return home.

At the beginning of 2010, my world had shattered. My brother had an unsuccessful hernia surgery. After several days on life support, he passed away. My mother left and went to Virginia to stay with a friend, and I returned to my best friend's home.

STUCK

Despite my bereavement, I finished my last year of high school. However, I didn't receive my high school diploma when I graduated. I was held back a year due to my P. E. sub skipping my name in the grade book.

In the summer of 2010, my best friend's mother couldn't care for me. I had to leave. My relationship with my mother was tumultuous at best. Nevertheless, we reunited and moved to Hartford, Connecticut.

Right before my 19th birthday, I left her. I had to make it on my own. We were homeless, living in a motel room again, and any chance she could get, she would berate me. She would make me feel like I should have been the one to die.

Money was a constant concern, and the fear of being without it haunted me. This fear led me to abandon my college education in 2016. My dream was to graduate college and earn a Bachelor's Degree in Music and Business Administration, but having no support made it difficult to accomplish.

At 25, I decided to pursue my passion as a songwriter, but my love and compassion for my mother held me

STUCK

back. She was homeless again, and I had a place. I was planning on moving out of state the following year. Therefore, I moved her in and stayed another year to put her on my lease. Boy, was that a stupid decision.

In 2018, she moved out, leaving me with a car I couldn't drive, which I totaled. Another setback, another hurdle to overcome. The confidence to embrace my identity as a talented songwriter finally dawned on me, only to be followed by digestive issues along with anxiety in 2019.

My life had been a series of setbacks and disadvantages, and by 25, I found myself stagnating for seven long years. But now, as I share my journey through "Stuck." I have found healing through the pages of this book, and I hope it can help you find your way, too.

Be free, my dear
Be you without fear

Thank You!

I AM VELLY VEL

The Spoken Word Artist

Follow me on
Tik Tok, Instagram, Facebook,
YouTube, & Pinterest
@bynupinkthewriter

Visit
www.bynupinkthewriter.com
For more contents

THIS IS ONLY THE BEGINNING!

Please research

Ego Evolution Theory

and

Maslow's Hierarchy of Needs

FEBRUARY 2025

Color of Love

POETRY TRILOGY

I love in the dark when
the morning rise.
He will never know
only when my pen
writes.

I chase the feeling
not the human
Yet, I am chasing him
to feel included.

Loving another him
will be priceless
But I rather love my
spirit, it's expensive.

www.ingramcontent.com/pod-product-compliance
Lightning Source LLC
Chambersburg PA
CBHW020743130626
46554CB00006B/2125